Genre > Drama

Essential Question
How do you decide what is important?

Odysseus
and
King Aeolus

A Play

retold by Karen Alexander • illustrated by Juan Caminador

ODYSSEUS AND KING AEOLUS

CHARACTERS

Leonidas *(lee-oh-N...)*
Grandfather
Corinna
Jason
Irene

PROPS NEEDED

- backdrop of a tr...
- toy horse
- toy ship

of cardboard
to create wind

THE TROJAN WAR

Leonidas and his cousins Nicolas, Irene, Corinna, and Jason are spending time with their grandfather, who tells them tales of their ancestors in ancient Greece. They enter, stage right, and join Grandfather, who is already sitting on the ground under a tree.

LEONIDAS: Grandfather, you promised you'd tell us about Odysseus today.

GRANDFATHER: I did, didn't I? Well, it was many years since Odysseus had left his home on the island of Ithaca in Greece to fight in the war against Troy. Odysseus hadn't wanted to leave. In fact, he had pretended to be ill so he wouldn't have to go to war. But when he did get to Troy, he fought bravely.

CORINNA: Tell us about the Trojan Horse.

JASON: What Trojan Horse?

IRENE: It was Odysseus's brainstorm. It worked, too!

NICOLAS: Shhh. Listen to Grandfather.

(Stagehands bring in horse, stage left, and place it at far stage right.)

GRANDFATHER: The war had dragged on for ten years. No one was winning, and many people had died. The Trojans were tired of war, and the Greeks wanted to go home.

One morning the people of Troy awoke to find all the Greek ships gone and a wooden horse outside their gates. They looked at it suspiciously. Several hours later, the horse was still there, and the Greeks were still gone.

(Trojan 1 and Trojan 2 enter, stage left, and cross the stage to look at the horse.)

TROJAN 1: They've gone. Their ships have gone, too. I think it's a peace offering.

TROJAN 2: Let's open the gates and drag it inside.

(They open imaginary gates, drag the horse inside, and carefully close the gates behind them. They look at the horse as Grandfather talks.)

GRANDFATHER: When the horse was inside the gates, the bottom opened and out climbed some Greek soldiers. The Trojans were alarmed—with good reason. The soldiers ran and opened the gates to let in the other warriors, who had been hiding.

LEONIDAS: (*interrupting Grandfather*) I thought you were going to tell us about Odysseus!

GRANDFATHER: Yes, you're right. The Trojan War lasted ten long years. Then it took Odysseus another ten years to sail home...

JASON: What was the Trojan War about, anyway? Did the Greeks win?

GRANDFATHER: That's a story for another day. Today, I'm going to tell you about one of the adventures Odysseus had on his long journey home.

(*Trojans exit, stage right, with horse.*)

THE KEEPER OF THE WINDS

Sailors enter, stage left, with ship. Sailor 1 is on lookout. Sailor 2 is steering, Sailors 3 and 4 are pulling down a big sail.

SAILOR 1: Land ahoy! Call Odysseus—I can see land.

SAILOR 2: It looks like a castle floating on the ocean.

ODYSSEUS: (*entering, stage right*) That's the island of Aeolia, where King Aeolus lives. The king is the Keeper of the Winds. The island floats, but it never floats away.

SAILOR 3: Can we land there?

ODYSSEUS: It'll be necessary to climb that bronze wall, but then we should be okay. The main problem will be whether the king will let us stay.

(*They all exit, stage right, with ship.*)

GRANDFATHER: Odysseus and his crew scaled the high walls that protected the island from invaders. They were warmly welcomed by the king.

CORINNA: I know the next bit: they spent a whole month resting and feasting before Odysseus decided it was time to get on their way again.

LEONIDAS: Yes, in exchange for the king's hospitality, Odysseus entertained the court with tales of his fantastic adventures.

(Sailors 2 and 3 enter, stage right. They sit to talk with one another. Odysseus and the king enter, stage right. They are walking backward and forward and talking.)

ODYSSEUS: I thank you for your hospitality, King Aeolus. This is a beautiful island, and you are lucky to possess it. However, I long to see my own island of Ithaca again.

KING AEOLUS: I'm sorry to see you go, Odysseus. I have enjoyed your company. But I have a gift that will help you on your way. You can consider it a reward for the wonderful stories you told. *(He hands over a bag. It is tied tightly at the top with a cord.)*

ODYSSEUS: Thank you, King Aeolus. It is generous of you to share your wealth with me.

KING AEOLUS: You are welcome, Odysseus. It is not wealth as most people would think of it, but I think you will find it is a far greater treasure than gold. You must not open the bag, but even so it will help you to sail swiftly back to Ithaca.

(They exit, stage right, followed by the sailors.)

HOMEWARD BOUND

All four sailors enter, stage right. One of them is carrying the bag. They are muttering to one another.

GRANDFATHER: Odysseus and his crew were delighted to find how smoothly their ship sailed homeward. The gentle west wind filled their sails, blowing them swiftly toward Ithaca.

(Stagehands use cardboard to create a gentle breeze across the stage.)

SAILOR 3: *(as if continuing a conversation)* We definitely heard the king tell Odysseus there was treasure in the bag.

SAILOR 2: Yes, and the king told Odysseus not to open the bag. I guess he didn't want Odysseus sharing the treasure with us.

SAILOR 4: You're obsessed! You've been talking about that bag for the whole journey. I don't believe there's anything important in it at all.

SAILOR 1: There's one way to find out. We could open the bag.

SAILOR 3: Odysseus told us under no circumstances to open the bag. Something bad might happen if we do.

SAILOR 1: Well, he's been steering the ship for nine days. He's exhausted. As soon as we spied Ithaca on the horizon, he went to sleep. Now is our chance.

SAILOR 4: But Odysseus has always treated us honestly. I don't believe he would lie to us or not share gold and silver with us.

SAILOR 2: I, for one, vote that we look inside the bag. If there's nothing exciting in it, there's absolutely no harm done, and Odysseus need never know. The fires of Ithaca are already in sight. We won't have another opportunity.

(The sailors peer eagerly into the bag. Immediately, strong winds blow on the sailors. They run off stage in terror, stage left.)

GRANDFATHER: The sailors decided to open the bag while Odysseus was sleeping. Out whooshed all the wild winds. King Aeolus had trapped the winds in the bag so that Odysseus would have an easy journey home. The winds caused havoc, blowing the ship this way and that. They created a great storm.

Odysseus was awakened by the noise. He and the sailors watched in anguish as the ship was blown farther and farther away from Ithaca.

RETURN TO AEOLIA

Sailors 1, 2, 3, and 4 enter, stage left.

Sailor 1 is on lookout. Sailor 2 is steering.
Sailors 3 and 4 are repairing the ship.

SAILOR 1: Land ahead! I think it's Aeolia again.

SAILOR 2 Yes, yes, it is! Odysseus, we can see land.

(Odysseus enters, stage right.)

SAILOR 3: At least we can be sure of a welcome on the island.

SAILOR 4: Yes, if it weren't that I long to see my family again, I'd be happy to settle there.

ODYSSEUS: Right; two of you come with me. We'll go and ask the king to help us again. You two *(pointing to Sailors 3 and 4)* keep on repairing the ship so that we can set sail as soon as possible.

(Sailors 3 and 4 exit, stage right. Odysseus and Sailors 1 and 2 exit, stage left.)

GRANDFATHER: But when Odysseus got to the king's house, he was not welcomed. In fact, the king was very angry.

(*King Aeolus enters, stage right. Odysseus and Sailors 1 and 2 enter, stage left.*)

KING AEOLUS: What are you doing here, Odysseus? You should be home by now.

ODYSSEUS: It is my fault, King Aeolus. My crew opened the bag and let loose the winds. We were blown all over the ocean before we again came to Aeolia. We need your help.

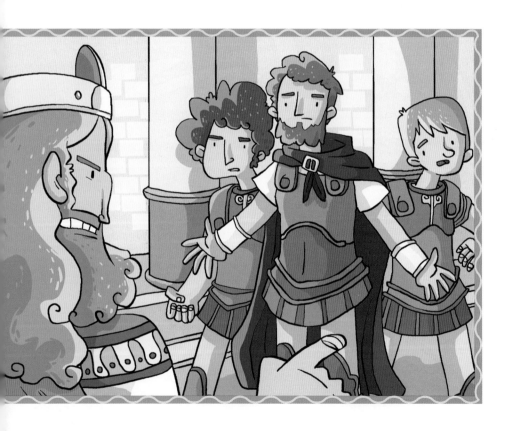

KING AEOLUS: I helped you once. The gods must be angry with you to have let such a disaster occur. I cannot help those whom the gods wish to harm. Get off my island!

(*Odysseus and the two sailors run off the stage, stage right. King Aeolus exits, stage left.*)

GRANDFATHER: With those words, the king had Odysseus and his men thrown off the island. They rowed for many days, until they were able to mend their sails. During that time, they met with other disasters and dangers. It was ten long years before Odysseus finally set foot on Ithaca again. On the way home, he had many more exciting adventures.

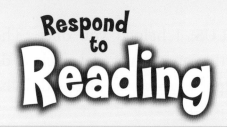

Respond to Reading

Summarize

Use details from the story to summarize *Odysseus and King Aeolus*. Your chart may help you.

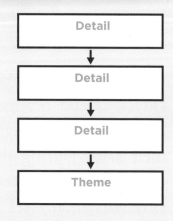

Detail
↓
Detail
↓
Detail
↓
Theme

Text Evidence

1. How do you know *Odysseus and King Aeolus* is a play and a myth? Name two things you notice about the text. GENRE

2. What happened to the gift that King Aeolus gave Odysseus? THEME

3. Find the word *imaginary* on page 4. What is the root word of *imaginary*? What do you think *imaginary* means? ROOT WORDS

4. Write about how the author communicates the theme, or message, in the play. WRITE ABOUT READING

Compare Texts

Read about a person who realizes what is important to her.

Daria's Dream

The school's annual cross-country race is about to start, and Daria can't wait. Daria loves sports and is great at track, but she has never done well at the cross-country race. The bumps and the uneven ground on the course slow her down. Her friend Alexis, on the other hand, nearly always wins. Daria is determined that this year is going to be different!

The last time Daria went to the eye doctor, she found out she is near-sighted. Now that she has glasses, Daria can see every rock, stone, and bump on the ground as she runs. For the past two months, Daria has trained extremely seriously for the cross-country. Her dream is to beat Alexis— just this once.

Illustration: Antonio Vincenti

17

Daria and Alexis start off together. Many of the other athletes start off by running as fast as they can. They quickly outstrip Alexis and Daria. However, the girls know what they are doing. If they want to last the distance and finish the race, they need to pace themselves.

As they get toward the end of the course, Daria and Alexis gradually overtake all the other runners. Some of them are still running steadily, but others are bent over and gasping for breath. Then, slowly, Alexis gains the lead. A few minutes later, Daria manages to pass her. Then Alexis gains on Daria again and passes her.

Around the next bend, Daria comes upon Alexis crouching on the ground.

"What's happened?" cries Daria.

"I twisted my ankle on a tree root," gasps Alexis, wincing in pain. "Don't stop; keep going!"

Daria hesitates.

"I'm fine," shouts Alexis. "Go on, Daria! Win for both of us."

Daria runs a few yards, but then she stops. She turns and comes back. "I'm staying with you until assistance arrives," she says. "I'd sooner lose the race with you than win it without you."

Make Connections

What does Daria decide is more important than winning the race? ESSENTIAL QUESTION

Compare how Odysseus and Daria each learn a lesson just before reaching an important goal.

TEXT TO TEXT

19

Focus on Genre

Plays A play is a story that is written to be performed in front of an audience rather than read. The text is mostly dialogue. The people who perform in a play are called actors. Stage directions describe what the characters do. Props, such as the ship and the horse in *Odysseus and King Aeolus*, also help make the story come alive. Plays have scenes instead of chapters.

Read and Find In *Odysseus and King Aeolus*, the names of the characters are written in upper case and bold. A colon separates the name of the character from the words that the character will speak. The stage directions are written in italics. These directions tell the characters what to do.

Your Turn

Write another scene for *Odysseus and King Aeolus*. It is set on board the ship after Odysseus and his crew have been thrown off the island of Aeolia. Remember to use text features to show which character is speaking and what each character is saying and doing.